To Shala

MW01531177

Thank so much for being a blessing to me! I love you & I pray overwhelming blessings for you & your family as well as your business!

Love ya!

Angela Washington

Empowered to Be Great Devotional

Greatness Is Your Divine Inheritance

∾

ANGELA M.
WASHINGTON

WESTBOW
PRESS®
A DIVISION OF THOMAS NELSON
& ZONDERVAN

This book is a work of non-fiction. Unless otherwise noted, the author and the publisher make no explicit guarantees as to the accuracy of the information contained in this book and in some cases, names of people and places have been altered to protect their privacy.

WestBow Press books may be ordered through booksellers or by contacting:

WestBow Press
A Division of Thomas Nelson & Zondervan
1663 Liberty Drive
Bloomington, IN 47403
www.westbowpress.com
1 (866) 928-1240

Because of the dynamic nature of the Internet, any web addresses or links contained in this book may have changed since publication and may no longer be valid. The views expressed in this work are solely those of the author and do not necessarily reflect the views of the publisher, and the publisher hereby disclaims any responsibility for them.

Any people depicted in stock imagery provided by Getty Images are models, and such images are being used for illustrative purposes only.
Certain stock imagery © Getty Images.

Scripture taken from the King James Version of the Bible.

Scripture quotations marked (NLT) are taken from the Holy Bible, New Living Translation, copyright © 1996, 2004, 2007 by Tyndale House Foundation. Used by permission of Tyndale House Publishers, Inc., Carol Stream, Illinois 60188. All rights reserved.

THE HOLY BIBLE, NEW INTERNATIONAL VERSION®, NIV® Copyright © 1973, 1978, 1984, 2011 by Biblica, Inc.® Used by permission. All rights reserved worldwide.

Scripture taken from The Message. Copyright © 1993, 1994, 1995, 1996, 2000, 2001, 2002. Used by permission of NavPress Publishing Group.

ISBN: 978-1-9736-9143-3 (sc)
ISBN: 978-1-9736-9142-6 (hc)
ISBN: 978-1-9736-9144-0 (e)

Library of Congress Control Number: 2020908170

Print information available on the last page.

WestBow Press rev. date: 05/19/2020

Contents

Preface

Empowered to Be Great Devotional was birthed in 2012, during a season of life during which I felt lost and confused about the direction God was taking me. Dealing with life after divorce was something that I was not prepared to handle with only my own strength. I had always been considered the "strong" one in the family. But even Jesus himself became weak! This season opened old wounds and hurts that I had thought were healed. I was going to divorce care, counseling, and psychiatric counseling. I knew God, but where was He? I knew the Bible verses, I knew songs that I could sing to help me make it through the day, and I knew how to pray. But I was so deeply hurt that I couldn't see or hear God, and honestly I didn't want to. I was angry at God for allowing this to happen to me. Yes, this Christian who loved God so much allowed Satan to really have his way then. That led down a path of anxiety, depression, and shortly afterwards to a suicide attempt. I spent five days in a mental hospital. Even though I didn't understand how I'd gotten there, I remember praying, "God, wherever You send me I'll go." The staff asked me why I was there. I answered that I was not sure, but I was going to be okay. At the time, I really didn't believe my own words. I had mandatory sessions every day, and I used vision boards to learn how I saw myself. I did that, but then I went back to my passion, which was journaling. That's when I began to write this devotional.

As I was riding home after being released from the hospital, I remember the trees and grass looking greener, the sky so blue and beautiful, and the sun shining so big and bright. In that moment I realized I was just existing, not really living. I recall one morning in my time with God when He said to me in all his sweet wonder, "I never left you." This bought me to tears, and I knew in that moment that God had kept me here for a reason, and I had to live. I fought for every moment and every day He woke me up. Some days were more challenging than others, but slowly and surely, as I walked with Him, things began to shift.

In 2013 I suffered great loss in my families, which opened my eyes. I began to live my life for real, because I realized it could be taken in a moment. At the end of the year, I began to consult God concerning jobs and where I should live. All on my opportunities came from Texas; even though it wasn't my first choice, God said something different. In 2014, I stepped out on faith and trusted God, moving to Dallas, Texas. This was the best decision I could have made, even though I didn't think so at first. I prayed and asked God to show me the way, guide my steps, and tell me what to or how to do it. Doors began to open. I found a church home, and things began to come together.

Fast-forward to 2018. One night I was looking for an old brochure I had for my business, and I stumbled across this "Day 1 Devotional." I called my best friend and asked her about it. She told me, "You did a lot of writing in 2012." I searched online but found nothing to link with what I had written. I prayed to God about my next move. He laid on my heart that I should search for Christian publishers, and that is how I got to this point. Now

I can officially deliver and present to you, *Empowered to Be Great Devotional: Greatness Is Your Divine Inheritance.*

Understand that we are created in the image of God. I believe He is great and that greatness is our inheritance. It is in our spiritual DNA. Everything that we need to succeed and live life more abundantly we already have. We must speak greatness into the atmosphere, speak it over our finances, our businesses jobs, and families. It is ours, and the power is in our voices.

Greatness Is Your Divine Inheritance

Definitions by Merriam-Webster Dictionary

Greatness: distinguished or eminent. **Synonyms:** Illustriousness, prominence, genius, caliber, distinction, finesse, proficiency, virtuosity

Inheritance: the reception of genetic qualities from parent to offspring. **Synonyms:** birthright, legacy, heritage, patrimony

Divine: linking to God. **Synonyms:** None

Key Scripture

And because you are sons, God has sent forth the Spirit of His Son into your hearts, crying out, "Abba, Father!" Therefore you are no longer a slave but a son, and if a son, then an heir of God through Christ. (Galatians 4:6–7 NKJV)

Most of the time when we think of an inheritance we think of money, property, or something that we receive from a family member who has passed away. Sometimes, when an heir cannot be located, the property will go to the state. I remember when I was growing up in Arkansas, at a certain time of the year on the state news there would be an announcement that people should contact the state or go to a website to claim their property.

With our Heavenly Father, there is no need to contact Him through a website. We must put God in remembrance of His promises to collect our inheritance. This inheritance is not new cars or more money coming our way. The inheritance we receive from God consists of spiritual blessings, gifts of the Spirit, and His unconditional love, grace, and mercy—things money cannot buy or our social status cannot get us. We are created in His imagine; before we were formed in our mother's wombs greatness was divinely deposited in our spiritual DNA. God planted the seed of greatness and fertilized it with His promises if we obey His voice and commandments.

> *And it shall come to pass, if thou shalt hearken diligently unto the voice of the Lord thy God, to observe and to do all his commandments which I command thee this day, that the Lord thy God will set thee on high above all nations of the earth: And all these blessings shall come on thee, and overtake thee, if thou shalt hearken unto the voice of the Lord thy God. Blessed shalt thou be in the city, and blessed shalt thou be in the field. Blessed shall be the fruit of thy body, and the fruit of thy ground, and the fruit of thy cattle, the increase of thy kine, and the flocks of thy sheep. Blessed shall be thy basket and thy store. Blessed shalt thou be when thou comest in, and blessed shalt thou be when thou goest out. (Deuteronomy 28:1–6 KJV)*

Angela M. Washington

He sealed it with His word, just as a good father would affirm his child.

> So be strong and courageous! Do not be afraid and do not panic before them. For the Lord your God will personally go ahead of you. He will neither fail you nor abandon you. (Deuteronomy 31:6 NLT)

Then God gives us an everlasting reminder of His stamp of approval, that greatness is our divine inheritance.

> For God so loved the world, that He gave His only begotten Son. That whosoever believeth in Him should not perish but have everlasting life. (John 3:16 KJV)

God gave His only Son, Jesus Christ, to die on the cross for our sins that we may have life and live more abundantly. People may count us out, but God never gives up on us. Greatness is not a choice for us; it is our only option. God did not design us to settle for mediocrity but to strive to embody all the greatness that He placed inside of us. He created us to bring Him glory and honor. God said in His word that if He be lifted up He will draw all men. He will use us to show others His love, grace, and mercy. He has equipped us from birth to succeed and to walk in divine favor and abundance. God desires that we take Him at His word. He has given us everything we need to live this life. I challenge all of us to pray bigger, dream bigger, believe bigger, and watch God work.

In whom also we have obtained an inheritance, being predestinated according to the purpose of him who worketh all things. (Ephesians 1:11 KJV)

Prayer

Father God, I take this moment in time to say thank you for our divine inheritance. Thank you for being our Heavenly Father. Daddy, there is no one like You anywhere. I love You, and I am so honored to serve You, Heavenly Father. Thank you for your promises. Help me, Holy Spirit, to obey the voice of God and His commandments. Help me insure that His will be done in my life, on earth as it is in Heaven. Father, activate my gifts and talents to do Your will and what You created me to do. Help me, that I may bring glory to Your name. Every idea, ministry, or business that You planted inside of me, God, activate it now; breathe life into it, and show me how to operate in it. God, You lead and direct, and I will follow; I am all Yours. And thank you for giving your son, Jesus Christ, to die on the cross for my sins. I am forever grateful for my divine inheritance. In Jesus's name, amen.

Notes

Angela M. Washington

Revive Me for My Purpose

Definitions

Revive: to reinstate consciousness or life; to reinstate from a depressed, inactive, or unused state; to reintroduce in the mind or memory. **Synonyms:** recharge, resuscitate, resurrect, renew, revitalize, rejuvenate, rekindle, regenerate, refresh, restart, reactivate

Purpose: the reason something is done or used: the goal or intent of something; the feeling of being strongminded to do or achieve something; the aim or goal of a person: what a person is trying to do, become, etc. **Synonyms:** ambition, meaning, dream, aspiration, plan, target, idea, aim, intention, ideal, point

Key Scripture

He has saved us and called us to a holy life—not because of anything we have done but because of his own purpose and grace. This grace was given us in Christ Jesus before the beginning of time. (2 Timothy 1:9 NIV)

In the beginning, God created the heavens and the earth (Genesis 1:1). We are all created for a purpose and with a purpose in mind. God had a purpose for us to be great, amazing, beautiful, and smart. We are love. We deserve to be loved. We are enough, and we are worth it. We will survive, and we will conquer giants. We will walk in victory and never be defeated. God thought enough of us to make us all these marvelous things and more. This happened long before we knew of Him and before we were getting to know Him. God knew us even before our parents knew about us; He knew who and what we would become. How cool is that! Yet life will throw us curve balls, packing a punch if we don't have what it takes: "You will never make it out of this situation. You will never get married. Your parents' marriage failed, and yours will too." The list of lies Satan will tell us goes on and on if we allow it to, and it will repeat in our family for generations to come.

> Thou wilt keep him in perfect peace, whose mind is stayed on thee: because he trusteth in thee. Trust ye in the Lord forever: for in the Lord Jehovah is everlasting strength. (Isaiah 26:3–4 KJV)

Satan is always on his job, and you need to always be on yours. Satan will use your family or closest friend to say something mean or hurtful. And you should have a scripture to give back. For example, If your "best friend" says, "You have never done anything like this, I think you need to do something else more your speed," the comeback scripture might be this one.

> Not at all! Let God be true, and every human being a liar. As it is written: "So that you may be proved right when you speak and prevail when you judge." (Romans 3:4 NIV)

Angela M. Washington

We can no longer live our lives without doing so on purpose. We must be intentional about all we do, where we go, who we talk to, how we treat one another, and who we share our dreams with. There are always what I like to call "dream snatchers." They are people who are lurking to see whose dreams they can destroy or who they can cause to have doubts or fears. There is one thing I have learned on this journey of life that stands true forever and always.

> And we know that all things work together for good to them that love God, to them who are called according to his purpose. (Romans 8:28 KJV)

Let us be intentional, to live on purpose and with the purpose that God created us for.

Prayer

Lord, thank you for creating me on purpose for the purpose that You have destined for me. With You, God, and through Christ, I can do all things that strengthen me. Father God, help me to accept the calling that You have placed on my life. Help me and show me, Holy Spirit, how to walk in the gifts You have graced me with. And show me how to live each day in my purpose with grace and ease. In Jesus's name, amen.

Notes

I'm Different

Definition

Different: partly or totally distinct in nature, form, or quality; not the same; unusual, special. **Synonyms:** non-identical, diverse, unalike, distinguishable

Key Scripture

You made all the delicate, inner parts of my body and knit me together in my mother's womb. Thank you for making me so wonderfully complex! Your workmanship is marvelous—how well I know it. You watched me as I was being formed in the utter seclusion, as I was woven together in the dark of the womb. You saw me before I was born. Every day of my life was recorded in your book. Every moment was laid out before a single day had passed. How precious are your thoughts about me, O God. They cannot be numbered! (Psalm 139:13–17 NLT)

This is one of my favorite passages in Psalms. It reminds us to be concerned for what God thinks about us, not what other people think. Life can be mean, and so can people. I knew I was different at an early age, when I was in third grade. I had just moved to a new state and a new school with new people. I was terrified, but nobody knew it. The girls bullied me because I had full lips. Being the new kid on the block didn't make it any better. But that was minor compared to the dreams the Holy Spirit gave me. I felt that I could never tell a soul, because I was afraid they would think I was crazy! I was scared to tell my parents, because growing up in the South and being a Baptist, I knew they were going to say I needed some spiritual counseling. And when my dreams became realities—just as I'd dreamed them—I had all kinds of thoughts at first that something was wrong, but I didn't feel weird. I knew I had to be special for God to show me these things, but at the same time I was afraid to embrace them or tell about them. I just supported everyone else. I stayed in the background and played the cheerleader. If a man or woman of God called me a dreamer, a prophetess, or a minister, I would be on the run! I put my track shoes on so fast you'd have thought they had wings and turbo boosters. "Thank you, but no. That's not for me. I am on a mission, but that's not it" would be my response to that.

But honestly, we all are ministers in some capacity. I remember that when I was a teenager, there was a young man who wanted to call me. I said that the only way we could talk was we had to read the Bible. A few months later, he saw my pastor and told him that because I'd given him the word, he'd given his life to Christ. I remember that the night when my pastor told me about it I prayed, and God said, "If you can save one, you can save a thousand, and if you can save a thousand, you can save ten thousand." Now that I am older and have gotten to know God for myself, I understand very well, and I welcome my difference. I understand just this:

> Though I am free and belong to no one, I have made myself a slave to everyone, to win as many as possible.

Angela M. Washington

To the Jews I became like a Jew, to win the Jews. To those under the law I became like one under the law (though I myself am not under the law), so as to win those under the law. To those not having the law I became like one not having the law (though I am not free from God's law but am under Christ's law), so as to win those not having the law. To the weak I became weak, to win the weak. I have become all things to all people so that by all possible means I might save some. I do all this for the sake of gospel, that I may share in its blessings. (1 Corinthians 9:19–23 NIV)

I say this often: this life we live is truly not our own. We go through things in life to be a testimony to someone else. If we just lift the name of Jesus, keep Him first in all that we do, He will do the drawing. I am reminded of an old hymn: "And if I, if I be lifted up, from the earth I'll draw all men unto me." Embrace your difference. As Christians, we are different and sometimes thought of as crazy, but this is a good thing. God set us apart for His glory. And don't be afraid to share your difference, because somebody has been waiting to see someone that looks just like them.

Prayer

Daddy, I love You so much. Thank you for making me special for Your glory. I ask Holy Spirit to show me how to embrace my callings, gifts, and talents so not a soul is lost to Christ because of my neglect. Holy Spirit, teach me how to walk boldly and unapologetically in my difference, not ashamed of the gospel of

Jesus Christ. Devil, you will not stop what God has ordained. I plead the Blood of Jesus over my mind, that I have the mind of Christ, because a double-minded person is unstable in all of his ways. God, I give You the honor and praise that is due to only Your name. I lift You, Lord, and magnify You. In Jesus's name, amen

Notes

God, I Trust You!

Definition

Trust: assured confidence on the character, ability, strength, or truth of someone or something; dependence on something future or contingent. **Synonyms:** credence, faith, stock

Key Scripture

Trust in the Lord with all your heart and lean not on your own understanding; In all your ways acknowledge Him, And He will direct your paths. (Proverbs 3:5–6 NKJV)

Trusting God can be difficult for some people. But it is vital to our very being to trust God. Trusting God may feel like testing our faith, our patience, our relationship with God, and other things we can think of when we are going through this greatest test. Trusting God takes everything we have, everything within us to keep going even when we cannot see clearly.

In late 2013, I lost my favorite aunt. She had only been fifty, and I'd never known her to take a vacation—she had eight weeks of paid vacation time left on her job. It was so unexpected, and it hurt me so deeply, because she'd been my friend, sister, and mother all in one. I began to pray about what God had in mind for me. I just didn't want to live my life without enjoying it or fulfilling God's purpose for me. Dallas had not been my choice to live, only to visit. I'd applied for jobs across the country, but most of my opportunities had come from Dallas, Texas. So I'd decided to come for one weekend, to just see where I would live if I chose to live here. I'd ended up staying the entire week and having four interviews. I said, "Okay, God, if this is where You have planned for me to be, I will move." I went back to Arkansas at the end of that week, packed up my little apartment, and made the move. It was a sudden one, but I knew my life depended on it.

> So Samuel said: "Has the Lord as great delight in burnt offerings and sacrifices, as in obeying the voice of the Lord? Behold, to obey is better than sacrifice." (1 Samuel 15:22 NKJV)

In January 2014, I packed my car and moved to Dallas. I didn't understand why God was sending me here, but He surely did. I remember crying as I crossed the state line and saying to God, "I trust You. I know You know what is best for me. I give You everything I have. I trust You." After I got here, none of the job interviews worked out. I was sleeping on the floor with an air mattress in my friend's one-bedroom apartment; I had very little money. But I knew what God had spoken to me. It was one of the loneliest seasons of my life, being the first time I had moved away from my family. But I trusted God, because truly that was all I had. My car never got repossessed, my insurance never lapsed, I never went hungry, my cell phone never got turned off, and I had shelter. I remember sitting on my air mattress one night and saying, "God, I think I made a bad decision. I am sure I heard You,

Lord. Why did You send me here? A month later I still have no job and no place of my own. Why?" And Holy Spirit, in all His sweetness, spoke to me, saying, "All I wanted was you." After I heard those words, the tears would not stop. I had to say, "God, I am so sorry. I do trust You!" Shortly afterwards, I obtained employment and got my own place.

> He says, Be still, and know that I am God. (Psalm 46:10 NIV)

We must get still, just stop sometimes. We are so busy trying to figure out what to do or how to fix the situation, when God has already worked it out. Trust God when He says, "I am." Trust God in who He is and always will be.

> Great is our Lord and mighty in power; his understanding has no limit. (Psalm 147:5 NIV)

God is everything we need—and more. I remember being in the Angel Choir at eight years old and singing this song: "He's Got the Whole World in His Hands." We must remember that He is the ultimate creator of all. If the birds of the air and the fish of the sea can trust the Creator to feed and supply their needs, why can't we? We cannot move our bodies or feel, smell, walk, talk, and see without God. We take the small things for granted, and we may forget to say thank you. But God always knows when to show up; He's never late. He will meet our needs wherever we are, even if we don't say thank you. Trust God. If He did something for us before, we can believe that He will do it again. Even when we cannot sense the presence of God, God is there. When we can't feel or hear God, we have to learn to open our Bibles to hear His voice. Trust God. He's the heavyweight champion of the world. He's never lost a battle, and He always keeps His promises. There is no failure in Him.

Prayer

Father God, thank you for teaching me that You have everything that I need. You—not my job, my people, or my parents—are my source. Thank you, God, for teaching me to trust You with what I already have, because that is all I need. Thank you for reviving my trust in You, and forgive me for ever doubting you. Help me, Lord God, to trust more and more each day. You said in Psalm 146:3, *"Do not put your trust in princes, in human beings, who cannot save."* So, God, I put all my trust in You, because I know you will never let me down. I know that in God there is no failure; You are not a man that you should lie. Thank you, Lord God, for always loving me and keeping Your promises. Lord, I praise you. You receive all the glory, honor, and praise. In Jesus's name, amen.

Notes

God, I Need Peace

Definition

Peace: a state of serenity or quiet; freedom from unsettling or unfair thoughts or emotions; on one accord in personal relations. **Synonym:** tranquility, calm

Key Scripture

Don't worry about anything; instead, pray about everything. Tell God what you need and thank him for all he has done. Then you will experience God's peace, which exceeds anything we can understand. His peace will guard your hearts and minds as you live in Christ Jesus. (Philippians 4:6–7 NLT)

Research has shown that women are more commonly afflicted by anxiety disorders than men. God made women so unique; he gave us wombs, which means we are created to be carriers. We are nurturers by nature; we care a little more about everything. We are intuitive on a whole other level, if we tap into it. I believe that is why when women are hurt, especially emotionally, it takes longer for us to get over it. We hold onto hurts that cause us to lose appetite, sleep, weight, and hair, and we suffer from migraine headaches and other physical ailments while worrying about things that we cannot change. We even have the nerve to worry about everyone else we are connected with. I am one of those people who just genuinely cares; I used to pick up everybody else's issues when they brought them to me. I would be restless, praying and worrying over them when they dumped their burdens on me, while they would be moving right along with life.

> Give all your worries and cares to God, for he cares about you. (1 Peter 5:7 NLT)

All we need to do is turn our burden over to Jesus and stop worrying about it. Easier said than done, some would say. I was one who was guilty of not always leaving it at the altar, and I am sure some of you can relate. God is not the author of confusion but of peace. There is nothing too hard for God. When life seems to get hard and we don't understand why, we must take it to the Lord in prayer.

> For God is not the author of confusion but of peace, as in all the churches of the saints. (1 Corinthians 14:33 NKJV)

> Ah, Lord God! Behold, thou hast made the heaven and the earth by thy great power and stretched out arm, and there is nothing too hard for thee. (Jeremiah 32:17 KJV)

Though confusion does not stop God from working, Satan will try his best to have it stop us. As I grew in my relationship with God, I really began to understand the old hymn "What a Friend We Have in Jesus." There is a portion of the song that says it is a privilege—an honor—to carry everything to God in prayer. It tells us that we forfeit our peace and allow needless pain, all because we choose to not carry everything to God in prayer. The song does not say "some things" but *everything*! We have to learn to pray about everything and not to worry about anything. God does not put more on us than we can bear. If we are feeling weighted down, maybe we have taken on things that God did not ordain. God is the Prince of Peace! His peace is like none other; it soothes all doubts, calms all fears. We sleep better when we are resting in the peace of God; we feel more positive and more uplifted. God is a peacemaker. We must pray about everything and leave it all at His feet. There is no problem too big or burden too heavy; God can handle it. Just give it to the Lord, and watch Him work.

Prayer

God, I come to You, thanking You, for You are my peace. I pray about everything and worry about nothing. I cast all my cares, my fears, my stresses, my concerns, my insecurities, my doubts, and my stressors over to You, Lord God. I know You can handle these far better than I ever can. Father, I thank You for showing how to let go and allow You to take care of me and the situations that I could not handle on my own. Lord, I bless You for showing me how to guard my heart and trust You. Lord God, I thank You and I honor You, for You are a healer, a restorer, a Mighty God, a Wonderful Counselor, and an Everlasting Father. You are a protector, a friend, the lover of my soul, and a comfort. In Jesus's name, amen.

Notes

Heal My Heart Condition

Definitions

Heal: to make free from injury or sickness; to be made complete or whole; cause to be overcome; to patch up or correct; to reinstate to original purity or integrity. **Synonyms:** cure, fix, mend, rehabilitate, set up

Heart: the emotional or moral nature different from the intellectual nature; such as generous temperament; love, affection, courage, or enthusiasm when maintained during a difficult state; one's innermost character, moods, or predispositions. **Synonyms:** bigheartedness, charity, compassion, commiseration, feeling, good-heartedness, softheartedness, mercy, pity, sympathy, warm-heartedness, kindliness

Condition: a state of presence; old fashioned. **Synonyms:** order, repair, shape, trim, kilter, keeping, health, form

Key Scripture

My flesh and my heart may fail, but God is the strength of my heart and my portion forever. (Psalm 73:26 NIV)

I am sure it is safe to say that we all have had our share of heartaches, disappointments, hurts, and an array of negative emotions. We sometimes find ourselves reliving these, because we have leased heart space for them to take up residence. This keeps us bound and on an endless emotional roller-coaster ride. I was going through a very tough time in my life; I had gotten divorced and wasn't sure what was next for me. I was so broken. I was looking for validation from all the wrong people, and that made things worse rather than better.

I recall a dream I had one night. I was lying on an operating table, as if I were asleep. But I could see in the dream the bruises and scars on my face and body, and my chest was black and blue. As the surgeon was beginning to open my chest, I woke up. God said to me, "I wanted you to see that no matter what, I can make you whole again. I am giving you open-heart surgery, because that is the only way that you can live again. I have to repair your heart, so that you can love again, trust again, be completely whole again, to receive love—true love—and know that you deserve it, daughter." Wow!

We never know how much damage we do to ourselves when we hold onto the hardships of life. But we quickly take for granted things we need that are right in front of us. What we allow to dwell on our minds will manifest in our hearts. We must control our thoughts, because we will unconsciously attract what we think we deserve, and it can become reality. We have all had to learn the hard way that we cannot just open our heart space for any and every person. Everyone does not have our best interests at heart. People will say, "I am praying for you" and all the while will be thinking of how they can sabotage you. Guard your heart as if your life depends on it—because it truly does.

Above all else, guard your heart, for everything you do flows from it. (Proverbs 4:23 NIV)

We need to allow God to heal every wound, every place we have ever been hurt. We must stop carrying the baggage of pain and allow God to make us whole again. Moving forward is a little easier when we are a little lighter.

Prayer

Lord God, thank you for healing my heart and making me whole again in You. Thank you for teaching me to love You again and trusting You again. Forgive me for thinking that You stopped loving me and that You were never there for me. Thank you, Father, for strengthening my heart to trust You. God, I will never let go of You again, because I know in my heart, in my mind, and to the depths of my soul that you will never let go of me. You will never stop loving me. I am eternally grateful for all You have done, are doing, and are about to do, on earth as it is in heaven. In Jesus's name, amen.

Notes

My Spirit Is Dying

Definitions

Spirit: a supernatural existence or core. **Synonym:** soul

Dying: approaching death; gradually ceasing to exist; having reached an advanced or ultimate stage of decline or neglect. **Synonym:** moribund

Key Scripture

Being confident of this, that he who began a good work in you will carry it on to completion until the day of Christ Jesus. (Philippians 1:6 NIV)

Life circumstances and experiences can cause us to be broken in spirit. Not having a relationship with God can cause a disconnection in spirit. I attended church all my life. I went to Sunday school, sang in the choir, taught Sunday school, and served as an usher. I went to Bible study, Baptist Training Union (BTU), and let me not forget the church district meetings and state conventions. But then I found that everything I thought I knew about God and church was being tested. I remember attending church once, out of obedience to what I had been taught. But I was spiritually dying. I thought my prayer life and relationship with God would sustain me. It was so bad that I let the devil win. I stopped going, the worst thing anyone can do. I felt as if I had completely walked away from God. I didn't want to pray, because I was angry with God because my marriage had ended, to be honest. But I got tired one day of the emptiness I felt in my heart, the longing and hunger for God's presence. I felt lost, lonely, and unfilled. I remembered that God is the source of our strength. His strength is made perfect in our weakness. Through prayer, devotion, worship, and asking for forgiveness, I found my way back to Him. I asked God, "Just do it again—revive my spirit, revive me again, God, for your glory. Please, I am begging; I need you." It was as if God was just waiting to hear me say those words. He began to minister to me, telling me to go and worship him in my "sanctuary," to close my eyes and just worship him as I'd done when it was just him and me. I might have to cry through it, but it was not about me anymore. I knew I could not live my life on my own terms and my own will, not without Jesus Christ. I had to move past myself. Somebody needs what we have.

For in him we live and move and have our being. (Acts 17:28 NIV)

This experience taught me that we must allow God to guide us to the right ministry for our souls' salvation. It's not because the church is a pretty building and we know everybody that attends, or because they help in community, or because everybody goes there. That is the church to go to if you want to feel important. Every table we put our feet under is not meant for us to eat from. In other words, every church may have a great ministry, but it may not be the ministry for every person. If the church does not grow us spiritually, stretch our faith, or make us strive to be better Christians, we may need to start talking to God about the best place to worship. For God to complete a great work in us, we must stay connected to the source and lifeline, Jesus Christ. How do we do that? Glad you asked.

First, read and study the Word of God.

> *Study to shew thyself approved unto God, a workman that needeth not to be ashamed, rightly dividing the word of truth. (2 Timothy 2:15 KJV)*

Second, have a prayer life. Set a time and place to pray in your home or a special place, like a park or on the lake, a place that brings focus, insight, and perspective.

> *Confess your faults one to another, and pray one for another, that ye may be healed. The effectual fervent prayer of a righteous man availeth much. (James 5:16 KJV)*

And lastly, connect with a church, one in which you can grow spiritually. And share your faith with others.

> *And they overcame by the blood of the Lamb, and by the word of their testimony. (Revelation 12:11 KJV)*

Prayer

Thank you, Heavenly Father, for restoring my soul and spirit to live for You. Thank you for making me whole and brand new. Forgive me for not being obedient to Your voice and Your commands. Thank you for always loving me. Satan, you are defeated, and all the victory belongs to Jesus. I will live for Christ, and my life will bring Him glory and honor. I will walk in obedience to God's will. Father God, I gird my loins with truth and put on the breastplate of righteousness; my feet, Lord, will be of preparation of the gospel of peace. I will carry the shield of faith everywhere I go, that I will be able to quench the fiery darts of the wicked, cover my head with the helmet of salvation, and carry the sword of the Spirit, which is the Word of God. Lord, I worship and adore You forever and always. In Jesus's name, amen.

Notes

Order My Steps, Lord

Definitions

Order: to put in order: arrange; to give an order to; command; destine, ordain; to command to go or come to a specified place; to bring about order; regulate. **Synonyms:** sequence, setup, arrangement, array, disposal, disposition, distribution, ordering.

Steps: a stage in a process; an action, proceeding, or measure often occurring as one in a series. **Synonyms:** expedient, means, measure, move, shift

Key Scripture

If you need wisdom, ask our generous God, and he will give it to you. He will not rebuke you for asking. But when you ask him, be sure that your faith is in God alone. Do not waver, for a person with divided loyalty is as unsettled as a wave of the sea that is blown and tossed by the wind. Such people should not expect to receive anything from the Lord. (James 1:5–7 NLT)

When we take any great step or make any decision, our focus must not be only on our immediate plans to build or establish. We should always use Godly discernment when making decisions.

The steps of a good man are ordered by the Lord: and he delighteth in his way. (Psalm 37:23 KJV)

Much of the anxiety and regret that come from the weight of our decisions can be alleviated or avoided if we assemble all our information and have the right knowledge. We must take time to focus on the far more difficult processes that will follow and the long-term consequences of our decisions.

For I know the thoughts that I think toward you, says the Lord, thoughts of peace and not of evil, to give you a future and a hope. (Jeremiah 29:11 NKJV)

We know and affirm that there is no such thing as a stupid question.

My people are destroyed for lack of knowledge. (Hosea 4:6 NKJV)

Our choices are no stronger than the facts we have. This requires information. We should never attempt to silence the voice within us that continues to question! God wants us to have knowledge. Learning to rely on the Holy Spirit for directions wasn't always easy for me. I wondered, *What's next? How is it going to work out?* and *How am I going to make it work?* But I am learning to truly ask for guidance and to be confident that the Holy Spirit is not going to lead me wrong.

The fear of the Lord is the beginning of wisdom, And the knowledge of the Holy One is understanding. (Proverbs 9:10 NKJV)

Angela M. Washington

It is a faith walk. Once I hear the voice of the Lord, I go and do. I trust him—with shaking knees and at times crying—but I close my eyes, breathe, and walk on the water. Often we think we know what is best for us. But God, the one who created us, knows us better than we know ourselves. I learned that what I thought I wanted wasn't what God had in store for me. He gave me what I wanted because we have permissive will and the perfect will of God. I never thought to stop and ask what his perfect will for my life was, out of fear of him telling me that my way was not what he wanted for me. I wanted what I wanted. That was before I began to really know who God was in my life. Since then my prayer is that God's will be done in my life.

We should pray and surrender our wills to God—our ways, our thoughts, our agendas, our opinions, our wants, our fears, our desires, everything—because we must desire to have God's best for our lives. Our lives are unto God. He gets the glory out of our lives; it is not about us. Nothing on this earth is about us; it is all about Him. So that we walk in the steps God has ordered for us, we must trust him.

Prayer

Lord, thank you for ordering my steps. Thank you, because I know now that You never have and never will lead me wrong. You are the director and compass for my life and my soul. Wherever you lead me, Father, I will follow. My decision is to follow You, Lord God. Guide me all the way; guide my thoughts that I think the right thoughts; guide my tongue that I say the right things; guide my footsteps that I won't go to places that I shouldn't. I can't do it without you. Lord, I praise You in advance, because I know that it is already done on earth as it is in heaven. In Jesus's name, amen.

Notes

God Is Water to Our Souls

Anyone who believes in me may come and drink!
For the Scirptures declare, "Rivers of living water
will flow from his heart." (John 7:38 NLT)

GOD IS WATER TO OUR SOULS

Water to the human body is the most important nutrient for
every function. Water is a lubricant; it flushes toxins from the

body and aids with digestion. Water is a huge component of blood, which carries oxygen to and from all cells. Water gives a moist environment to all the tissues of the body.

God is water to our souls. Just as we need water for our physical bodies, the Word of God provides nutrients and moisture to our spiritual bodies. God quenches our everlasting thirst, the thirst for Him. God is the only one who fills every void we may have in our lives. God is water to our souls.

God is a healer. If I had never been sick, hurt to the point of attempting suicide, or just down and unsure how I was going to get back up—if I'd never suffered anxiety, depression, or rape—I would never have known that God is the healer who is water to our souls.

God is a keeper. He will sustain us. When our physical bodies are weak, He is strong in us. He will give us strength to endure and carry out the assignments that He has placed on us, in us and for us. God will keep us even if when we don't want to be kept and forget that He is doing just that already! God is a keeper, just like water to our souls.

Because He Lives

Definition: None needed

Key Scripture

Praise be to the God and Father of our Lord Jesus Christ! In his great mercy he has given us new birth into a living hope through the resurrection of Jesus Christ from the dead. (1 Peter 1:3 NIV)

We are all familiar with the old hymn that says, "Because He lives, I can face tomorrow. Because he lives, all fear is gone. Because I know He holds the future. And life is worth the living, just because He lives."

Because Christ lives, we can face tomorrow. That means that no matter what happened today, yesterday, last week, last year, or thirty years ago, we can face tomorrow. Because Christ lives inside of us, we can rest assured that he is going to take care of us. We can trust him.

> *Give your entire attention to what God is doing right now, and don't get worked up about what may or may not happen tomorrow. God will help you deal with whatever hard things come up when the time comes. (Matthew 6:34 MSG)*

Because Christ rose from the dead with all power and authority, and he lives inside of each of us, we can face life with power and authority over Satan. We can stop letting Satan torment us mentally, emotionally, health wise, financially, in our jobs, in our homes, in our families, and in our marriages. God has given us authority, because He lives. This scripture states it best:

> Behold, I give you the authority to trample on serpents and scorpions, and over all the power of the enemy, and nothing shall by any means hurt you. Nevertheless do not rejoice in this, that the spirits are subject to you, but rather rejoice because your names are written in heaven. (Luke 10:19–20 NKJV)

We must daily submit our will, our wants, our desires, our agendas, our thoughts, and our ways to God, so that are completely dependent on God. Because Christ lives, all anxiety is gone from us.

> Say to those with fearful hearts, "Be strong, and do not fear, for your God is coming to destroy your enemies. He is coming to save you." (Isaiah 35:4 NLT)

It doesn't matter what Satan throws our way to make us frustrated and fearful. Christ has paid the price. When we are fearing a situation or are emotional challenged, we can know that God is fighting for us. We must remind ourselves of this scripture:

> For God has not given us a spirit of fear but of power and of love and of a sound mind. (2 Timothy 1:7 NKJV)

When the spirit of fear comes upon us, we know for sure that it is not from God. Therefore, we must begin to pray immediately for God to remove fear and let His light shine on the space the darkness is trying to fill. Because we know that Christ holds the future and life is worth living just because Christ lives. We can rest secure in knowing this.

> *Being confident of this very thing, that He who has begun a good work in you will complete it until the day of Jesus Christ. (Philippians 1:6 NKJV)*

Christ has already given to us everything we need to live this life and live it abundantly. We must trust the Holy Spirit in us; God is going to see us through and fulfill every promise.

Prayer

Holy Spirit, thank you so much for being my comforter and my guide. Because Jesus Christ lives, I can face tomorrow. I ask, Holy Spirit, that You strengthen my heart, that I may trust you to see me through, no matter what. I know that there is nothing too hard for You, God. You can do the impossible. Let Your light shine on me and through me, that when others see me they see Your life, God. Because Your life is light. I love You; I worship You and You alone. There is none like You, Lord, in all the earth. Satan, you get no glory and no praise. All victory belongs to Jesus. In Jesus's name, amen.

Notes

Delayed
but Not Denied

Definitions

Delaying: postponing, hampering, or causing something to take more time than normal **Synonyms:** holding pattern, holding back, waiting, detainment, detention

Deny: to declare false, to not to admit or acknowledge, to not to accept as reality or fact. **Synonyms:** disallow, disown, disaffirm, contradict, reject, negate, refute, disavow

Key Scripture

I say to myself, "The Lord is my inheritance; therefore, I will hope in him!" The Lord is good to those who depend on him, to those who search for him. (Lamentations 3:24–25 NLT)

Have you ever prayed for something and it seemed as though God did not hear you? We have all felt that at some point in our lives. God is always working on our behalf. He never sleeps; He never slumbers. Even when we think God is not speaking, He is still working and speaking. All we have to do is pick up the Bible, and there are words from the Lord on every page. When we cannot trace God, that is when we should activate our faith and trust Him even more!

> Trust in the Lord with all heart; do not depend on your own understanding. Seek his will in all you do, and he will show you which path to take. Don't be impressed with your own wisdom. Instead, fear the Lord and turn away from evil. (Proverbs 3:5–7 NLT)

God is never late; He is always on time. God's timing is not our timing. Can you think of something that you prayed to ask God for, but it didn't come about as you had prayed for? Do you remember how you felt, how disappointing it was, the sacrifice you'd made for it that maybe no one else knew about? I am reminded of this scripture:

> "My thoughts are nothing like your thoughts," says the Lord. "And my ways are far beyond anything you could imagine. For just as the heavens are higher than the earth, so my ways are higher than your ways and my thoughts higher than your thoughts." (Isaiah 55:8–9 NLT)

We can ask God again; we may be delayed but not denied. We must believe that God is the answer. Why not ask Him, if He has all the answers and He is the answer? We must thank God for the delays also, because some delays are for our good. Think about the times when we were supposed to leave the house to go somewhere and were running ten minutes late. Then we discover that there was a car accident just minutes prior, on the route to our destination. Therefore we had to take a detour to get where we were going. Some delays are God's protection. We can think about a few more things God delayed that saved our lives. God knows what we need and when we need it. We may not understand the delay regarding our prayers, but we must learn to ask when we pray that God will strengthen our hearts to trust Him. Our delay is not denial but the glory for our patience in waiting on God.

Prayer

Father God, I thank You for sometimes putting me in a holding pattern. Thank you for teaching me that Your ways and your thoughts are higher than mine, God. Thank you for being a good father, a father who cares and loves me enough to correct me. God, I ask that You forgive me for every time I thought I knew what was best for me and did not need you. But most of all, thank you for never denying me Your love, God. You never disowned me. In Jesus's name, amen.

Notes

Call His Name

Definitions

Call: to say something in a loud voice so it can be heard at a distance; to make an appeal or petition. **Synonyms:** cry, note

Name: a word or phrase that distinguishes the difference of a person or thing; a person or thing with a status; family; one referred to. **Synonyms:** esteemed, prestigious, recognized, reputable, respected, respectable

Key Scripture

The name of the Lord is a strong fortress; the godly run to him and are safe. (Proverbs 18:10 NLT)

When we first meet someone, we are greeted, followed by the person's name. There is meaning to our names, and believe it or not, this is often reflected in our personalities and characters. I can recall a certain tone that my parents used to let my siblings and me know when we were in trouble or something was urgent. It sure got our attention quickly! That is exactly how it is with God. When we, his children, call His name, He knows our voices, and we get His attention immediately. God is—He is just that! I am so in love with just that: "God is." We know that there is power in the name of Jesus. Demons tremble at His name. There is no greater name than the name of Jesus, which can heal any sickness or disease, can raise the dead, can mend a broken marriage, can give hearing back to the deaf, and can open blinded eyes. This scripture says it best:

> For a child is born to us, a son is given to us. The government will rest on his shoulders. And he will be called: Wonderful, Counselor, Mighty God, Everlasting Father, Prince of Peace. His government and its peace will never end. He will rule with fairness and justice from the throne of his ancestor David for all eternity. (Isaiah 9:6–7 NLT)

When we need someone to talk to, or when we need a lawyer in the courtroom, He's that kind of wonderful counselor. When we need God to fight for us, He is Jehovah Nissi, "The Lord is our banner."

> Moses built an altar and called it The Lord is my Banner. (Exodus 17:15 NIV)

When it seems we are all alone, God is Jehovah Shammah, "The Lord is there."

> The distance all around will be 18,000 cubits. And the name of the city from that time on will be: The Lord is there. (Ezekiel 48:35 NIV)

When we are faithless, God is still faithful. He is El Emunah, "The Faithful God."

*Know therefore that the Lord your God is God; he
is the faithful God, keeping his covenant of love to a
thousand generations of those who love him and keep
his commandments. (Deuteronomy 7:9 NIV)*

Just when we think we don't have enough, God always make a way out of no way. Why? Because he is Jehovah Jireh, "The Lord will provide."

*So Abraham called that place The Lord Will Provide.
And to this day it is said, "On the mountain of the Lord
it will be provided." (Genesis 22:14 NIV)*

When the enemy try to make us doubt that God is God, that our God is a part-time God, remember that God is El Olam, "The Everlasting God."

*Lord, you have been our dwelling place throughout all
generations. Before the mountains were born or you
bought forth the whole world, from everlasting to
everlasting you are God. (Psalm 90:1–2 NIV)*

Life's pressures can sometimes weigh us down with sleepless nights and our hearts overwhelmed, but God is Jehovah Shalom, "The Lord of Peace."

*So Gideon built an altar to the Lord there and called it
The Lord Is Peace. To this day it stands in Ophrah of the
Abiezrites. (Judges 6:24 NIV)*

There is no other God like our God; just call his name. He is "the Most High God"; He is El Elyon.

I cry out to God Most High, to God, who vindicates me.
(Psalm 57:2 NIV)

Trust God in his I am–ness. There is nobody like our God. As we grow deeper in our relationship with God, we continue to learn the many names of God and use them in our prayers. The scriptures say that every knee must bow and every tongue confess that Jesus Christ is Lord. Jesus is Lord; He is the answer and He is the only way.

Prayer

Everlasting Father, I thank You, for You are great and greatly to be praised. You are awesome, amazing, excellent, and powerful. There is no other name that can heal the sick, raise the dead, and still do miracles, signs, and wonders today. Thank you for being my Jehovah Jireh, my provider. Thank you for being my Jehovah Nissi, for fighting for me. Thank you for being my Jehovah Rapha, my healer when I am sick. Thank you for being my Jehovah Shammah, always there for me, and thank you for being my Jehovah Shalom, my God of peace, giving me peace in my darkest hour. God, I honor You, I bless You, I magnify You. You reign, and you are Lord of my life. I love You and adore You so much. In Jesus's name, amen.

Notes

God Will Provide

Dedicated to my parents,
Mr. and Mrs. Arnell Washington

Definition

Provide: to make something accessible to, to stock or make obtainable. **Synonyms:** give, hand, hand over, feed, furnish, supply, deliver

Key Scripture

That is why I tell you not to worry about everyday life—whether you have enough food and drink, or enough clothes to wear. Isn't life more than food, and your body more than clothing? Look at the birds. They don't plant or harvest or store food in barns, for your heavenly Father feeds them. And aren't you far more valuable to him than they are? Can all your worries add a single moment to your life? And why worry about your clothing? Look at the lilies of the field and how they grow. They don't work or make their clothing, yet Solomon in all his glory was not dressed as beautifully as they are. And if God cares so wonderfully for wildflowers that are here today and thrown into the fire tomorrow, he will certainly care for you. Why do you have so little faith? So don't worry about these things, saying, "What will we eat? What will we drink? What will we wear?" These things dominate the thoughts of unbelievers, but your heavenly Father already knows all your needs. Seek the Kingdom of God above all else, and love righteously, and he will give you everything you need. So don't worry about tomorrow, for tomorrow will bring its own worries. Today's trouble is enough for today. (Matthew 6:25–34 NLT)

God is our Jehovah Jireh: "Our Lord will provide." We can all think of times in our lives when we were desperate for God to make a way; we had needs that nobody but God could fulfill. All we knew to do was to trust God, knowing that he would come through. Since he had done it before, he would do it again.

I grew up in a household of six people. If my family was poor, my mom and dad sure did not let us know it. We always had food on the table, clothes on our backs, shoes on our feet, and a roof over our heads. My mom and dad had more jobs than anyone I knew, not including all the work they did for our church, both local and state. My dad had a full-time job, and he was the bus driver, the janitor, and the lawn mower for the church as well as for a local restaurant and an elderly neighbor down the street. My mom was an entrepreneur of many trades, from owning a child-care business to being a caterer, wedding coordinator, seamstress, wedding/funeral program designer, and full-time employee.

I remember when the local supermarket had sales on, for example five cans of corn for a dollar. (Of course, they don't have sales like that anymore, anywhere!) My mom would send all four us into the store to each get five cans of corn. Our house was at times everybody's house, it seemed. Whether it was one of our friends, someone in the community, or a student from the school, if they were hungry, my mom would feed them. Our parents trusted God, and he multiplied what we had so that we never went without and had enough to be a blessing to others. I believe my parents, like so many of us now, just believed in this scripture:

> Even strong young loins sometimes go hungry, but those who trust in the Lord will lack no good thing. (Psalm 34:10 NLT)

My siblings and I never heard our parents complain. Of course we saw them get tired, but we never knew the sacrifices they made. My parents did teach us to read the Word of God and to stand on His promises. As an adult, I remind myself of this when times get hard:

> For the Lord God is our sun and our shield. He gives us grace and glory. The Lord will withhold no good thing from those who do what is right. (Psalm 84:11 NLT)

God always provides. Trust God, my brothers and sisters. God is a promise keeper; believe Him and believe in Him. God is not a liar; His Word still stands true. There is nothing that our God cannot do. He knows what we need before we need it.

> And my God will meet all your needs according to the riches of his glory on Christ Jesus. (Philippians 4:19 NIV)

Receive it, and thank God as if you already have it; it is already done. On earth as it is in Heaven. God provides!

Prayer

Holy Spirit, I thank You for reminding me that I serve Jehovah Jireh, "the Lord will provide." Thank for reminding me that in Christ there is no lack or want. I bind the spirit of poverty and lack off my entire bloodline, and I release the spirit of abundance and overflow. Thank you, Heavenly Father, for making ways for me, even in my unbelief when I didn't trust you. Forgive me for not trusting God. Thank you for restoring my faith in You. Thank you for providing for my family, taking care of all their needs and desires. I love You, Heavenly Father, and I trust you more today than I did yesterday. Strengthen my heart, that I will continue to trust You more and more each day. I know that whatever I need, You have promised in your Word that you will supply. I worship You and adore You. In Jesus's name, amen.

Notes

Freedom in Christ

Definition

Freedom: the value of being free, such as deliverance from slavery or limitation or from the power of another, the value being exempt; released, usually from something burdensome. **Synonyms:** independency, liberty, self-determination, self-governance, sovereignty

Key Scripture

So if the Son sets you free, you will be free indeed. (John 8:36 NIV)

We have all been bound by sins of some type. These might be generational curses, lies that we have told about ourselves and believed, the lies Satan has told us about ourselves, things that someone else has said to us, thoughts in our minds, or other things. These things have held some us captive for most or all of our lives. Can you imagine being held prisoner in your mind over something that was not true or real—and not just for a couple of hours, a day, or a year but for a lifetime? Some of us have been told, "You will never amount to anything! Your father was a drunk and your grandfather was one, and you are going to be one too" or "Your mother never graduated from high school, and your grandmother was a teen mother, and you will be the same way." Generational curses *can* be broken! When we begin to discover who we are in God and who God is in our lives, we can apply what the Bible teaches us to every curse and lie that Satan tries to defeat us with.

> *It is for freedom that Christ has set us free. Stand firm, then, and do not let yourselves be burdened again by a yoke of slavery. (Galatians 5:1 NIV)*

We are no longer bound; no more chains hold us. We are free in Christ. Christ went to the cross and gave his life so that we may live more abundantly. Sometimes we allow stress and the pressures of life to drag us down to the point that we cannot enjoy life anymore. We find ourselves with health issues because of it, on medication just to help us cope with life. But there is freedom in Christ, brothers and sisters. We must pray and seek God's directions. This scripture gives us hope, I believe.

> *No temptation has overtaken you except what is common to mankind. And God is faithful; he will not let you be tempted beyond what you can bear. But when you are tempted, he will also provide a way out so that you can endure it. (1 Corinthians 10:13 NIV)*

There are steps to finding freedom in Christ. The first step is prayer.

> *In my distress I prayed to the Lord, and the Lord answered me and set me free. (Psalm 118:5 NLT)*

The second step is love.

Angela M. Washington

For you have been called to live in freedom, my brothers and sisters. But don't use your freedom to satisfy your sinful nature. Instead, use your freedom to serve one another in love. (Galatians 5:13 NLT)

And lastly, know that freedom is found in your calling.

The Spirit of the Lord is upon me, for he has anointed me to bring Good News to the poor. He has sent me to proclaim that the captives will be released, that the blind will see, that the oppressed will be set free, and that the time of the Lord's favor has come. (Luke 4:18–19 NLT)

We are free in Christ. No matter what we have done in our past, the skeletons that we will take to our graves, or the demons that we fight daily, God is still on the throne and on our side. Christ went to the cross to die for not one or two or three of our sins but for *all* our sins. We must repent and know that once we repent and ask God for forgiveness, He throws our sins into the sea of forgetfulness and remembers them no more.

Prayer

Most Almighty God, first I say thank you for giving your only begotten Son, Jesus, to die on the cross for my sins. Thank you, Father, for giving me freedom in You. Forgive me for all my sins, both known and unknown. I repent now for being disobedient to You when you told me to do something and I didn't do it. For not trusting You and Your timing in my life, forgive me, Lord. Thank you for remembering those times no more. Thank you for the freedom in you, God, that I can live this life and live it more abundantly. Thank you for the freedom to speak of Your great name everywhere I go that souls are set free. For I am no longer bound; no more chains or shackles hold me. I am free to be who You created me to be for you, God. I desire for You to please be with me, Lord, in all that I do. I love You, thank You, honor You, worship You and You only. Thank you, God, for the freedom to lift my hands to you and to call upon your great name. In Jesus's name, amen.

Notes

God's Love

Definition

Love: strong affection for another arising out of relationship or personal ties; the object of appreciation; selfless loyal and compassionate concern for the good of another, such as the caring concern of God for humankind; friendly concern for others; a person's admiration for God; Eros. **Synonyms:** affection, attachment, devotion, fondness, passion.

Key Scripture

Love is patient and kind. Love is not jealous or boastful or proud or rude. It does not demand its own way. It is not irritable, and it keeps no record of being wronged. It does not rejoice about injustice but rejoices whenever the truth wins out. Love never gives up, never loses faith, is always hopeful, and endures through every circumstance. Prophecy, speaking in unknown languages, and special knowledge will become useless. But love will last forever! (1 Corinthians 13:4–8 NLT)

Love is amazing. The love of God is truly so. I never thought I would know God or his love in this way. As mentioned previously, I went to church, Sunday school, and so on when I was growing up. But I did not have a relationship with God until much later in life. I was baptized at an early age, as most of us are. But my idea

Empowered to Be Great Devotional   55

about God was this mean, angry, fire-and-brimstone, jealous man with hair like wool, a you-sin-or-even-think-about-it-you're-going-to-hell kind of God. And as I got older, I started seeking God for myself. I remember after graduating high school, I thought I was grown and decided I would move back to Texas. It was the worst decision I could have made at the time, but my parents, didn't stop me. I remember one night around 11:30 I was so lonely as I sat in bed. I said, "God, I miss my daddy. I really miss him." I had never missed my father in that way. It was in that moment that I felt the presence of God. Like a Heavenly Father, He came in and hugged me; I physically could feel him hugging me. That was the moment I fell in love with God.

> *We know how much God loves us, and we have put our trust in his love. God is love, and all who live in love live in God, and God lives in them. (1 John 4:16 NLT)*

My life from that moment has never been the same. My love for God increased even more. If you don't know about the love of God, I dare you to just try it today. God will forever transform your life.

There was another time in my life when I had to rely on the love of God to get me through the darkest and hardest place ever. I'd been living my perfect life, I thought. God had blessed me. Things were going well. I was so happy and in love, and then life happened. No one ever gets married to get divorced. I was crushed, ashamed, angry, and confused. I questioned everything I knew about God. It didn't matter to me that I had gone to church all my life, sung in the choir, knew how to pray, or had learned the Word of God. How could God allow this to happen to me? Eventually I became depressed, even attempting suicide. I had never thought I would come to that place. But when I arrived at the mental hospital that evening, a former prayer partner from my old church was the head nurse for my floor. God will send you an angel just when you need to see his light shine. In my room, I kneeled at the side of my bed, and I cried. I sang the chorus, "Oh, how I love Jesus; oh how I love Jesus; oh how I love Jesus; because he first loved me." That is when I realized that it was because Jesus loved me—me! This was not because I had been good or perfect or had obeyed God; it was nothing that I had done. It was unconditional love.

> *And as we live in God, our love grows more perfect. So we will not be afraid on the day of judgement, but we can face him with confidence because we live like Jesus here in this world. Such love has no fear, because perfect love expels all fear. If we are afraid, it is for fear of punishment, and this shows that we have not fully experienced his perfect love. We love each other because he loved us first. (1 John 4:17–19 NLT)*

Through it all I never stopped loving God, because I knew he would never give up on me; He never stopped loving me. I have come to know that God is a gentle giant, sweet but firm and fair. God is love! Who wouldn't serve a God like this? Who wouldn't love a God like this? What an amazing, loving savior. The love of God trumps everything—every sickness, every hurt, every pain, loneliness, insecurity, doubt, and fear.

Prayer

Heavenly Father, thank You today for Your love, Your kindness, Your grace, and Your mercy. Thank you, Master, for nobody can love me the way you can. Thank you for my parents, my family, and their love—which cannot be compared to Yours. Thank you for healing every wound in my past that almost made me give up on love, and thank you also for restoring me and making me whole again so I could love again. Continue to teach me to love Your way, Holy Spirit, because my way of loving sometimes comes with conditions. I want love God's way, pure and holy; that way I may bring glory and honor in all that I do. Teach me to love even when I don't agree, when I am angry, or when my heart is sad or hurt. I know, Lord, that Your love can heal, move mountains, restore, and conquer anything. Thank you for the strength now to trust You. Lord God, I thank You, love You, magnify You, worship You, and adore You. In Jesus's name, amen.

Notes

Who Am I?

Definition: None needed

Key Scripture

But as many as received him, to them gave he power to become the sons of God, even to them that believe on his name: Which were born, not of blood, nor of the will of the flesh, nor of the will of man, but of God. (John 1:12–13 KJV)

Who am I? is a question we have all asked ourselves or been asked at some point in our lives. We have all experienced situations that made us question ourselves, and we may have even questioned God, as if maybe He didn't know either. Statistics say that our names say something about who we are. The type of words we use when speaking, our handwriting, our perfume or cologne, and our eye color all say something about who we are. But what does God say about who we are?

> *See what great love the Father has lavished on us, that we should be called children of God! And that is what we are! The reason the world does not know us is that it did not know him. (1 John 3:1 NIV)*

I have learned on my journey to not give so much power to people. I do not allow people to tell me who they think I am. I thank God that I no longer look for others to validate me or give me permission to be the person He has called me to be.

We must seek God for ourselves and digest what His Word says about who we are. We should dwell on the things that God has downloaded to our spirits. The only one we should be looking for approval from is Him. He is the Alpha and Omega, the beginning and the end. He is the author and finisher of all things.

Every day we need to build our faith muscles; we must be ready always with the power and authority that God has given us. Let's remind Satan that God did not make a mistake in creating us. When Satan comes to sow doubt in our minds about who we are, we can simply use this strategy to decree over ourselves:

> I knew you before I formed you in your mother's womb. Before you were born I set you apart and appointed you as my prophet to the nations. (Jeremiah 1:5 NLT)

> And you are complete in Him, who is the head of all principality and power. (Colossians 2 NKJV)

> In righteousness you shall be established; You shall be far from sin, for you shall not fear; And from terror, for it shall not come near you. (Isaiah 54:14 NKJV)

Angela M. Washington

We know that whoever is born of God does not sin; but he who has been born of God keeps himself, and the wicked one does not touch him. (1 John 5:18)

But you are a chosen generation, a royal priesthood, a holy nation, His own special people, that you may proclaim the praises of Him who called you out of darkness into His marvelous light. (1 Peter 2:9 NKJV)

In Him we have redemption through His blood, the forgiveness of sins, according to the riches of His grace. (Ephesians 1:7 NKJV)

There is power in the Word of God but most of all power in the name of Jesus. We are considered deadly weapons to the power and principalities of the wicked when we know in God who we are. So let us be mindful that we desire to be what God called and created us to be. That is who we are.

Prayer

Lord Jesus, I come humbly to You, saying thank you for making me who I am. Thank you for always through your Word reminding me that I was fearfully and wonderfully made. God, forgive me when I doubt who You called me to be and made me to be. Now I walk boldly in my calling to win the lost, to witness for You, to bring You glory in all that I do, to minister to the masses and testify of Your goodness. Thank you, Heavenly Father, for Your grace and mercy. Satan, I am no longer bound and defeated by fear, anxiety, depression, insecurities, or doubt. I am who God says I am. I am more than a conqueror; I am of a royal priesthood. Wealth and riches are in my house. I am the head and not the tail; I am the lender and not the borrower; I am above and not beneath. Lord, I love You and praise You. I lift your name on high; there is none like You in all the earth. None can compare to You, Father. In Jesus's name, amen.

Notes

Angela M. Washington

Help My Unbelief

Definition

Unbelief: doubt or uncertainty, especially in matters of religious faith. **Synonym:** disbelief

Key Scripture

But Thomas, sometimes called Twin, one of the Twelve, was not with them when Jesus came. The other disciples told him, "We saw the Master." But he said, "Unless I see the nail holes in his hands, put my finger in the nail holes, and stick my hand in his side, I won't believe it." Eight days later, his disciples were again in the room. This time Thomas was with them. Jesus came through the locked doors, stood among them, and said, "Peace to you." Then he focused his attention on Thomas. "Take your finger and examine my hands. Take your hand and stick it in my side. Don't be unbelieving. Believe." Thomas said, "Master! My God!" Jesus said, "So, you believe because you've seen with your own eyes. Even better blessings are in store for those who believe without seeing." (John 20:24–29 MSG)

Sometimes we are just like doubting Thomas. Because we cannot see it, we don't believe that God is truly working on our behalf or that He is going to bless us as his Word promises. If we are honest with ourselves, before we grew as Christians, we sometimes struggled with questions like these: Is God real? Is He really this God that I hear my parents talk about? Is God really this God that I hear my grandparents talk about? Who is this God that I hear these people talk about in church? Is He real? I recall a preacher telling me that this God would never leave me nor forsake me. But then I lost my grandmother when I was nine and my favorite aunt when I was thirty-four. They had been like second mothers to me and my friends. I'd been able to talk to them about anything. It was the saddest and loneliest time, and for a while I wondered where God was.

When I was younger, before my brother and I moved permanently to Arkansas, our parents were struggling to make ends meet, and we lived in hotels. We had very little money, only the clothes we wore, and sometimes lived on food from convenience stores. When we did have a home, we would only live there for a short period of time, because we could not afford it. When my brother and I were with our father in the summertime, he taught us about God, taking us to church and Sunday school. We knew that God would always make a way and that He was faithful. When we went back to Dallas, we went to school, but we often arrived late because we had to depend on someone else to take us; we had no car. I remember my brother and I would say, "God, we are hungry," but we weren't sure whether we could still eat. We would go to the cafeteria long after breakfast was over, and the ladies were kind enough to give us breakfast. This reminds me of this sweet passage, because that was all we had and all we needed.

He replied, "Because you have so little faith. Truly I tell you, if you have faith as small as a mustard seed, you

Angela M. Washington

can say to this mountain, 'Move from here to there.'
And it will move. Nothing will be impossible for you."
(Matthew 17:20 NIV)

We must equip ourselves with the Word of God to empower us when we doubt what God can do for us. Questioning our God is exactly what Satan wants us to do! If we give Satan an inch, he'll try to become the ruler. We know our God is stronger, our God is real, our God is mighty, our God is El Elyon. He is God Most High, and He is Elohim, God is Mighty and Supreme. We become weak and want to faint, because we have not been conditioning our faith muscles by reading and studying the Word of God. Just as we go to the gym to condition our physical bodies for good health and to look our best, we should do the same for our spiritual bodies.

> *Your word is a lamp for my feet, a light on my path.*
> *(Psalm 119:105 NIV)*

Another way to condition our faith muscles is through prayer and fasting.

> *Then I set my face toward the Lord God to make request*
> *by prayer and supplications, with fasting, sackcloth,*
> *and ashes. (Daniel 9:3 NKJV)*

> *And I will give you the keys of the kingdom of heaven,*
> *and whatever you bind on earth with be bound in*
> *heaven, and whatever you loose on earth will be loosed*
> *in heaven." (Matthew 16:19 NKJV)*

And lastly, to condition our faith muscles we must give God thanks and praise.

> Enter with the password: "Thank you!" Make yourselves at home, talking praise. Thank him. Worship him. (Psalm 100:4 MSG)

> Be cheerful no matter what; pray all the time; thank God no matter what happens. This is the way God wants you who belong to Christ Jesus to live. (1 Thessalonians 5:16–18 MSG)

The following is our prescription for curing any unbelief that may flare up. Let us be found daily witnessing for Christ, conditioning our faith muscles, reading, studying the Word of God, praying, fasting, and giving God thanks and praise. We may be the only Bible that some people ever read. We must represent Christ well and bring Him glory in all that we do and say. I can hear my mom saying, "Only what you do for Christ will last."

Prayer

Father God, thank you for never leaving. Even in my moments of weakness and unbelief, You never gave up on me. I ask Your forgiveness, Father, for not believing that You had my best interest at heart, that You were going to provide for me, that You were going to protect me, and that You were able to accomplish all this. You said in Jeremiah 29:11 that You know the plans You have for me. You plan is to prosper me and not to harm me. Lord, I ask that You continue to strengthen my heart so that I trust You more today than I did yesterday. Help me to study Your word more, that I will continue to make room for You in my life and pray more. I want more of You and less of me. I don't trust me, but God, I trust You with my whole heart. Lord, I give You glory, and I pray that You get the glory for my life and all my acts. Everywhere I go I pray to represent You well, Lord. I love, I exalt, I give you honor, I give you praise. There is nobody like You, God, in all the earth. In Jesus's name, amen.

Notes

Forgiveness

Definition

Forgiveness: the end to feeling bitterness against, to give up hatred of, allowing space for error or weakness. **Synonyms:** absolution, amnesty, pardon, pardon, remission, remittal

Key Scripture

But when you are praying, first forgive anyone you are holding a grudge against, so that your Father in heaven will forgive your sins, too. (Mark 11:25 NLT)

Forgiveness can be hard no matter who we are. We can attend church all our lives, know the Bible, know how to pray and love God with all our hearts, but still find forgiveness a challenge. Some of us have been holding onto grudges for decades, not speaking to our siblings over things they said or did. We may hold onto resentment over something that a friend said or did years ago, while they may not even be aware that they offended us. But still we avoid them. Some of us have witnessed or experienced resentment and grudges that have kept people from apologizing to someone who has since passed away. This can be difficult to handle. But we serve a God who can heal and restore our hearts.

Bear with each other and forgive one another if any of you has a grievance against someone. Forgive as the Lord forgave you. (Colossians 3:13 NIV)

Let's look at one of the famous biblical stories on forgiveness, that of Jacob and Esau in the book of Genesis. These two were twins with very different personality traits. Esau was a man's man; he loved outdoor activities like tending the sheep and hunting. Jacob, on the other hand, loved to stay at home and learn from his mother.

One day when Jacob was cooking some stew, Esau arrived home from the wilderness exhausted and hungry. Esau said to Jacob, "I'm starved! Give me some of that red stew!" (This is how Esau got his other name, Edom, which means "red.") "All right," Jacob replied, "but trade me your rights as the firstborn son." "Look, I'm dying of starvation!" said Esau. "What good is my birthright to me now?" But Jacob said, "First you must swear that your birthright is mine." So Esau swore an oath, thereby selling all his rights as the firstborn to his brother, Jacob. Then Jacob gave Esau some bread and lentil stew. Esau ate the meal, then got up and left. He showed contempt for his rights as the firstborn. (Genesis 25:29–34 NLT)

The trickery continued. When their father, Isaac, knew he was near death, he requested that his manly son, Esau, kill some wild game to prepare a fine meal before dividing the estate. Rebekah, the mother of the twins, heard the request and helped Jacob pull off a grand arrangement to fool Isaac into giving Jacob the larger portion of the inheritance (Genesis 27). In the end, Jacob had to

Angela M. Washington

run for his life. He fled to another country to find his mother's relatives, who would care for him. It was many years before he returned to his own family. When he did, he heard that Esau was looking for him. Jacob the prankster—the deceiver—was scared. After all he had done, Jacob still tried to devise a plan so that his brother could only destroy half of his wealth if he caught him (Genesis 32). When they finally met, Esau ran to Jacob. He hugged him and kissed him and showed him forgiveness and mercy, just as Christ did us and advised Peter to do.

> Then Peter came to him and asked, "Lord how often should I forgive some who sins against me? Seven times? "No, not seven times," Jesus replied, "But seventy times seven! (Matthew 18:21–22 NLT)

Esau had forgiven Jacob, and he was surprised that Jacob would even think there was a grudge held between them. When we have the love of Christ in us, it is easy to forgive.

If there is something or someone that we have not asked God to forgive us for, now is the time to do so. Unforgiveness can wreak havoc on our health, mentally, emotionally, spiritually, and physically. Now is the time to forgive, to pick up the phone and schedule a lunch date with that person, or send some flowers and follow up with a visit or a card. It's time to pray and ask the Holy Spirit to show us how to approach the situation and make it right with ourselves and with God. If He forgives us for our sins and wrongdoings, can we do less? Satan would like us to dwell on our sins and will play on our emotions. But God's Word says that He will not remember our transgressions; it will be as if we never did anything wrong. Let us be encouraged and know that God forgives us many times; we should have the same heart to forgive and remember it no more.

> *"I, even I am He who blots out your transgressions for my own sake; And I will not remember your sins. Put me in remembrance; Let us contend together; state your case, that you may be acquitted." (Isaiah 43:25–26 NKJV)*

Prayer

Holy Spirit, thank you today for teaching me how important it is to forgive. Thank you for forgiving me when I made mistakes, when I disobeyed you, when I didn't trust you, when I did things my way, and when I walked in fear and doubt instead of faith and humility. Thank you for never letting me go. Continue to teach me how to forgive, because sometimes it gets hard and I want to do it my way. But Your ways, Lord, are better than my ways, and Your thoughts are better than my thoughts. Forgive me for the times I delayed in forgiving when I should have forgiven immediately. Thank you, Father, for forgiving me my sins, both known and unknown, and for remembering them no more. Continue to teach me to be a better disciple, a better servant, and a better witness for you. Lord, I pray I bring You glory, honor, and praise with all I do and say. I know I may not get it right, but help me and continue to show me Your way. In Jesus's name, amen.

Notes

Victory Belongs to Jesus

Definitions

Victory: the conquering of an enemy or adversary, achievement of proficiency or success in a struggle or endeavor against all odds or difficulties. **Synonyms:** success, triumph, win

Belong: to be fit, appropriate, or beneficial; to be in a proper condition; to be the property of a person or thing; to be committed or destined by birth, faithfulness, or reliance. **Synonym:** fit

Key Scripture

When you go to war against your enemies and see horses and chariots and an army greater than yours, do not be afraid of them, because the Lord your God, who brought you up out of Egypt, will be with you. When you are about to go into battle, the priest shall come forward and address the army. He shall say: "Hear, Israel: Today you are going into battle against your enemies. Do not be fainthearted or afraid; do not panic or be terrified by them. For the Lord your God is the one who goes with you against your enemies to give you victory." (Deuteronomy 20:1–4 NIV)

With Jesus Christ there is no defeat, no matter what Satan bring our way. We may buckle at the knees a little bit but never let the devil see us sweat. The ultimate battle was fought on the cross, and Jesus won! But in the New Testament Jesus performed many miracles just to remind us that the victory belongs to Him. And if He did it back then, He can do it again. Jesus raised Jairus's daughter back to life.

> While he was saying this, a synagogue leader came and knelt before him and said, "My daughter has just died. But come and put your hand on her, and she will live." When Jesus entered the synagogue leader's house and saw the noisy crowd and people playing pipes, he said, "Go away. The girl is not dead but asleep." But they laughed at him. After the crowd had been put outside, he went in and took the girl by the hand, and she got up. News of this spread through all that region. (Matthew 9:18, 23–26 NIV)

Jesus is still healing; he is still performing miracles, signs, and wonders, despite the conditions we see in newspapers, on TV, and on social media. Victory still belongs to Jesus; He still reigns and rules. Jesus healed many sick in Gennesaret when they touched His garment—another victory!

> When they had crossed over, they landed at Gennesaret. And when the men of that place recognized Jesus, they sent word to all the surrounding country. People brought all their sick to him and begged him to let the sick just

touch the edge of his cloak and all who touched it were
healed. (Matthew 14:34–36 NIV)

There are many miracles that we count as victories for Jesus in the Bible. We can take a moment and reflect on the many miracles that Jesus has performed in our own lives and the victories that we can credit only to Him.

But thanks be to God! He gives us the victory through
our Lord Jesus Christ. Therefore, my dear brothers
and sisters, stand firm. Let nothing move you. Always
give yourselves fully to the work of the Lord, because
you know that your labor in the Lord is not in vain. (1
Corinthians 15:57–58 NIV)

Prayer

Sweet Heavenly Father, thank you for every miracle, sign, and wonder that You have performed in my life, known and unknown. God, I give You the honor, because I know that each and every victory belongs to You, not because I have been good but simply because You are good! Thank you for helping Your people to see that You are still God despite what we see in the media and what we hear about you. We know that You are real and if it were not for You we would not be here today and we would not have the things or the privileges we have; we still bear witness to Your great and awesome name. We are not ashamed of You, God, and never will be. We stand up for You because You always stand up for us. Satan, has been and always will be defeated. He gets no glory or space in our lives. We plead the blood of Jesus over our families, finances, households, jobs, minds, bodies, schools, land, and country. It all belongs to God. Lord, we thank You, love You, magnify You, adore You, worship You, and exalt You. In Jesus's name, amen.

Notes

Angela M. Washington

Rejoice!

Rejoice always. (1 Thessalonians 5:16 NKJV)

REJOICE

We should rejoice in the Lord always. No matter what life throws our way, we must know that with Christ we can rejoice. God never makes a mistake. God knows exactly what we can handle and what we cannot. We must find peace in knowing that God has our lives and the world all in the palm of His hand.

Rejoice in the good times and even in the times when we don't understand what God is doing. We need to just lift our hands, give God praise, and rest assured that He is in control. Some may say this is easier said than done. That is true for some people, but others of us know that the God we serve is a mighty God of valor. He fights for us, He protects us, He provides for us, and He is always available to us.

Rejoice, my friends! There is freedom in rejoicing in the Lord. Once we have prayed about whatever it is, we owe God our praise, as it is already done and worked out in our favor. God wants us to cast all our cares on Him. There is no problem too hard for God to solve. Knowing that God cares that much about us should be enough in itself to cause us to rejoice!

Angela M. Washington

Be Sober

Definition

Sober: frugal in the use of food and drink, not drunk by intoxicating drink; serene; unhurried, calm; marked by abstinence, self-control, seriousness; to be subdued in tone; showing no extreme potential of fancy, emotion, or prejudice. **Synonyms:** clearheaded, straight

Key Scripture

Be alert and of sober mind. Your enemy the devil prowls around like a roaring lion looking for someone to devour. (1 Peter 5:8 NIV)

The devil is always busy; he is always up to something, seeking out someone who maybe wavering in faith or not sure in his or her salvation. Maybe he is looking for that person who is battling something in his mind. You see, the devil can slide in anywhere, even through a tiny pinhole. The devil is cunning, smooth, and a trickster.

> *Put on the whole armor of God, that you may be able to stand against the wiles of the devil. For we do not wrestle against flesh and blood, but against principalities, against powers, against the rulers of darkness of this*

age, against spiritual hosts of wickedness in the heavenly places. (Ephesians 6:11–12 NKJV)

In this hour we must stay sober and focus on what God is speaking to our hearts through our spirits. We must seek the voice of God for direction and stay alert, that we may carry out each step and stay the course in the vision that God gives us. We must not let the devil frustrate us, convince us we are losing our minds, put us under stress, cause us panic attacks, or disrupt our rest or our lives with foolishness. We must stay focused.

If God has given you a desire to start your own business, then pray. Ask the Holy Spirit to show you how to start it and do it. If God has given you a desire to apply for a better opportunity in your current job, pray and ask the Holy Spirit to show you what to do or who to talk to. Go for it! Whatever God have given you the desire to do, there is a reason that He has done this. You are created for far more than you think!

> *God can do anything, you know far more than you could ever imagine or guess or request in your wildest dreams! He does it not by pushing us around by working within us, his Spirit deeply and gently within us. (Ephesians 3:20 MSG)*

Stay sober! Stay vigilant!

Prayer

All-wise God, thank you for knowing what I need and when I need it. Thank you for keeping me calm and focused to hear Your

Angela M. Washington

voice and receive Your directions for my life. Forgive me when I get in Your way and my own. Thank you, Lord, for getting me back on track when I do fall off. Thank you for always loving me and for correcting me when I am wrong, because that is what a good father does. Continue to help me, God, to stay sober and vigilant as I walk in the steps that You have ordered for my life. Help me continue to trust You and ask You to show me the way, because my life is not my own—it belongs to you, Lord. Everything I have and everything I am belongs to you. God, I love You, I praise You, I lift You up, and I magnify Your name. My heart belongs to You. You are everything to me, God, and I honor You today. In Jesus's name, amen.

Notes

I'll Wait

Definition

Wait: To be in a place of expectancy; to remain fixed in readiness; to look forward eagerly; to be equipped and available. **Synonyms:** delay, detainment, detention, holdback, holding pattern, holdup

Key Scripture

As for me, I look to the Lord for help. I wait confidently for God to save me, and my God will certainly hear me. (Micah 7:7 NLT)

Many times we get frustrated while waiting for our food in the drive-through, waiting in line at the bank to cash our checks, waiting to pay for our groceries, lining up in the carpool line to pick up our children from school, waiting for the traffic light to turn green so we can get to our destination, or waiting in the security line at the airport. There are several things that we can think about until we find ourselves getting frustrated to no end. And honestly, we can't do anything about these things that are beyond our control.

I have officially relinquished my "superhero" powers. You know we all have them, the invisible powers, so that we think we can move traffic, get out of trouble, clean the house every day, get the children off to school every day on time, get to work on time, pick the children up from school on time, go grocery shopping, pay all the bills, take care of the world, and do it all over again every day for the rest of our lives—those powers! That is not real. There is only one God, and the last time I checked he was not taking applications for an assistant. But His Word does remind us of this:

> But those who trust in the Lord will find new strength. They will soar high on wings like eagles. They will run and not grow weary. They will walk and not faint. (Isaiah 40:31 NLT)

The reason we have become such a frustrated and stressed-out generation is that we have forgotten where our strength comes from and who is our help. We depend on our jobs, other people, and ourselves to do what only God can do. Meanwhile, God is sitting back and saying, "I'll wait." God is waiting on us to call on him for help. God is waiting for us to just say, "God, I need you" and "I can't do this anymore. This is too much for me to handle." God has all power. There is nothing so hard that God cannot handle it. There is no problem that is too difficult for Him. There is no sickness that God cannot heal. God is just waiting for us to turn it over to Him. He wants us to depend on Him again, to become like children to Him again. No matter what our age, we are always children to God.

> So the Lord must wait for you to come to him so he can show you his love and compassion. For the Lord is a faithful God. Blessed are those who wait for his help. (Isaiah 30:18 NLT)

Prayer

Lord God, thank you for waiting for me. Thank you for teaching me how to wait for You. Forgive me for the times I became impatient, took matters into my own hands, and You had to come rescue me. Thank you for never turning Your back on me and loving me despite my choices. Thank you for helping me to relinquish my superhero powers; You are the only super one. None can be compared to You, oh God. I can't do anything without You. I can't walk, talk, breathe, live, touch, see, or eat, and the blood that flows through my veins does so because of You. Every time I feel my pulse, I feel the love that You have for me, God, and for that I say thank you. God, I adore You, praise You, and exalt You and You alone. In Jesus's name, amen.

Notes

I've Got Joy!

Definition

Joy: an emotion aroused by well-being, success, or good fortune or by the vision of possessing what one desires; expression or demonstration of such emotion; a source or cause of delight **Synonyms:** beatitude, blessedness, bliss, blissfulness, felicity, gladness, happiness

Key Scripture

You will show me the path of life; In your presence is fullness of joy; At Your right hand are pleasures forevermore. (Psalm 16:11 NKJV)

Think of a moment in life when you experienced overwhelming joy—joy that flooded your soul, that brought tears to your eyes and great laughter to your entire being. That's it. That's the kind of emotion that is hard to explain to some. You can't explain it to someone who has never experienced it. It's just like that saying "You can't miss something that you never had." Joy is not like happiness. Happiness is based on what is happening. We depend on our money, life circumstances, achievements, marital status, social relationships, neighbors, and some researchers say genetic makeup to determine our level of happiness. But joy will stay with us always. All it takes is a memory, and the feeling comes right back to us. Jesus taught us well about joy when he spoke to the disciples in the New Testament.

> *These things I have spoken to you, that My joy may remain in you, and that your joy may be full. (John 15:11 NKJV)*

Joy makes us feel that we can conquer anything. With God on our side, we *can* conquer anything! No matter what the day brings, we've got joy! Stress? We've got joy! Depression? We've got joy! The bank account may be low, or the change is strange, but we've got joy! The bills are due, we've got joy! Sickness is trying to attack our bodies, but we've got joy! The refrigerator looks a little empty, but we've got joy!

> *Nehemiah said, "Go and enjoy choice food and sweet drinks, and send some to those who have nothing prepared. This day is holy to our Lord. Do not grieve, for the joy of the Lord is your strength." (Nehemiah 8:10 NIV)*

We cannot do anything on our own strength, even though we often think we can. God is the only one who can handle everything that life throws at us. There is nothing that our God cannot handle or fix. Nothing is too hard for Him. That is why we can have joy if we take everything to God in prayer. This doesn't mean a few things or just the little things, but everything—even the things that some of us intend to take to our graves. Yes, those things too! Everything is to go to God in prayer. There is no reason for us to lose sleep anymore. We can rest in the Lord and know that He will take care of us. We've got joy, and God's joy is everlasting.

Angela M. Washington

Prayer

Lord God, thank you for everlasting joy. Thank you for the rollercoaster ride, God. You taught me to lift my hands to You, to let go and to shout for You to help me. Forgive me for not depending on You and trusting You to take care of me. Daddy, I love You forever and always. You mean the world to me. Thank you for flooding my soul with overwhelming joy and peace as no one else does. Lord, I praise You, I adore You, and I worship You. You deserve all the glory and honor. In Jesus's name, amen.

Notes

Thank You

Definition

Thank you: a gracious expression of one's appreciativeness.
Synonyms: none found

Key Scripture

Enter with the password: "Thank you!" Make yourselves at home, talking praise. Thank him. Worship him. (Psalm 100:4 MSG)

Some of us were taught that when someone does something nice for us we say thank you. A thank you is simple, but it can be difficult for those who were never taught to say it or even think it necessary. But when it comes to the goodness of our God, we shouldn't have a problem telling Him thank you. God is good to us not because we've been good but because *He* is good. Sometimes we still don't thank Him. God allows danger seen and unseen to pass over us, and we don't say thank you. God is faithful when we are faithless, but we often don't think to stop and thank Him. In the book of Psalms, David provides us with instructions on how to thank and praise God for all things and how to show Him adoration for everything.

> *Let us come before his presence with thanksgiving and make
> a joyful noise unto him with psalms. For the Lord is a great
> God, and a great King above all Gods. (Psalm 95:2–3 KJV)*

Then we your people, the sheep of your pasture, will praise you forever; from generation to generation we will proclaim your praise. (Psalm 79:13 NIV)

I will praise the name of God with a song and will magnify him with thanksgiving. (Psalm 69:30 KJV)

If we take time to study the book of Psalms, it will help us be more thankful for everything that God has done and will do. We should thank God that His will for us will be done on earth as it is in heaven, in our lives, in our homes, on our jobs, in our businesses, and for our churches, our friends, our nation, our schools—just for everything under the heavens.

Prayer

Daddy, thank you! Thank you for all You have done. Forgive me for all the times that I didn't say thank you. If I had never been sick, I wouldn't have known that You are a healer. Thank you. If I had never had a broken heart, I wouldn't have known that You are a restorer. Thank you. If I had never been without food, money, or a place to sleep, I wouldn't have known that You are a provider. Thank you, Lord, for always being who You are, for never changing, for keeping Your word, and for always loving me unconditionally. With the lifting of my hands and my heart filled with praise for You and You alone, God, I say thank you. In Jesus's name, amen.

Notes

Amazing Grace
and Mercy

Definitions

Amazing: causing surprise or great wonder. **Synonyms:** astounding, dumbfounding, eye-opening, flabbergasting, jarring, jaw-dropping, jolting, shocking, stunning, stupefying, surprising, astonishing

Grace: unmerited divine support given to human beings for their renewal or sanctification; a virtue coming from God. **Synonyms:** favor, benevolence, boon, courtesy, indulgence, kindness, service, goodwill

Mercy: a blessing of divine favor or compassion. **Synonyms:** charity, clemency, forbearance, lenience, lenity, compassion, leniency

Key Scripture

Let us then approach God's throne of grace with confidence, so that we may receive and find grace to help us in our time of need. (Hebrews 4:16 NIV)

Let us take a moment and think about a time in our lives when we knew that, if not for the grace of God, we would not be, as some would say, on this side of the dirt. We have all been disobedient to our parents in some way, and we have all been disobedient to God, when he gave us instructions to do something and we didn't do it because we had our own agendas. Our parents may have been punished or disciplined us. But God spares us. His grace and mercy are so amazing! We don't deserve it, but God is such a good father. When we fall short, God picks us up, dusts us off, and gives us grace and mercy to start over again—and again and again. God gives us chance after chance. We've gone to places that we shouldn't have gone. We have been in relationships that we shouldn't have been. We have allowed our emotions to drive us to do things completely out of the will of God. Remember when God had to remind Paul about His grace, when he felt a thorn in his flesh?

> *But he said to me, "my grace is sufficient for you, for my power is made perfect in weakness." (2 Corinthians 12:9 NIV)*

As we look back over our lives, we can recall countless examples of God's amazing grace and mercy. We can even look down our entire family bloodline and see God's amazing grace and mercy at work. We see how God made a way out of no way. How God opened doors that only He could open and closed some that needed to be closed. How he provided for the family. How he kept us from all hurt, harm, and danger, seen and unseen. How when the doctors said, "We've done all we can do," God's grace stepped in.

From his life experiences, John Newton wrote one of the greatest hymns of all times in 1779; it is about the grace of God.

Amazing grace, how sweet the sound
That saved a wretch like me;
I once was lost, but now I'm found,
Was blind but now I see.
'Twas grace that taught my heart to fear,
And grace my fears relieved;
How precious did the grace appear
The hour I first believed.
When we've been there ten thousand years,
Bright shining as the sun,
We've no less days to sing God's praise
Than when we first begun.

Prayer

God, thank you so much for Your astounding favor and leniency.
I thank You for protecting me and keeping me, even when I didn't
want to be kept. Thank you for Your grace and mercy in showing
up right on time. Forgive me when I walk in disobedience to Your
will because I want to do things my way and not Yours. Thank you
for being a good father, for picking me up and dusting me off every
time in fail. Thank you for every chance that You have given and
continue to give daily. Lord, You are holy, You are wonderful, You
are amazing, and beside You there is no other. You are excellent,
You are magnificent, and I say thank you. In Jesus's name, amen.

Notes

Lord, I'm Available

Definition

Available: present or ready for immediate use; accessible, obtainable; qualified or willing to do something or to assume a responsibility. **Synonyms:** accessible, acquirable, attainable, obtainable, procurable

Key Scripture

And so, dear brothers and sisters, I plead with you to give your bodies to God because of all he has done for you. Let them be a living and holy sacrifice—the kind he will find acceptable. This is truly the way to worship him. (Romans 12:1 NLT)

I am reminded of a song I started singing in the youth choir in my church when I was growing up. It said, "Lord, I'm available to you, My will I give to you, Lord, I will do what you say do, If you just use me, Lord to show somebody else the way. My storage is empty to you, Father, and I am available to You."

To be accessible to God takes some sacrifice, and there can be moments when we feel all alone. As Christians, we have learned that surrendering our lives over to God wholeheartedly is a daily task. God is not just within the four walls of an establishment of worship.

God has called us to go out to reach the lost, those who have left the church for whatever reason, those who feel that God has forgotten about them, and those who feel all hope is gone. Therefore we must go out and be the billboard or megaphone for God. Sometimes we are the only Bible that others will read. We would not be where we are if not for God giving up Jesus Christ to die for our sins, for our parents taking us to church, or for our grandmama praying for us. We are nothing without God. The things that God has placed inside of us are not for keeping to ourselves.

> *God saved you by his grace when you believed. And you can't take credit for this; it is a gift from God. (Ephesians 2:8 NLT)*

God tells Christians not to be afraid of what the world is going to say. He calls us back to praying and seeking Him. God wants us to make room for Him in our lives. We have become so busy in our lives that we have forgotten who gave life to us. God is calling us to bring attention back to Him. The things that are taking place in the world today can be changed. We as Christians are the catalysts for change.

> *If My people who are called by My name will humble themselves, and pray and seek My face, and turn from their wicked ways, then I will hear from heaven, and will forgive their sin and heal their land. (2 Chronicles 7:14 NKJV)*

> *Seek the Lord while He may be found, Call upon Him while He is near. (Isaiah 55:6 NKJV)*

Being available to God requires us to become completely sold out for Him, so that our lives and entire beings belong to God for his glory. Being available requires us to say yes! Giving God our yes changes everything. When we say yes to God, we are saying, "God, I am submitting to Your will and to Your way for life. I will trust You every day for the rest of my life and will serve you." We tell God, "Yes, I'm available," even when we don't feel like it. That's because there is someone out there in the world who has been waiting on us, maybe to save a life, to heal a broken heart, or to soothe a sin-sick soul and mind. Someone may be waiting to hear how God changed our lives, because that person is ready to make a change. There are souls who are waiting on us, brothers and sisters. What will be our response? Are we ready to give God our yes? Are we ready to say, "Lord, I'm available to You; use me as you please."?

Prayer

Lord God, I come to You today saying thank you for giving Your very best to save someone like me. Forgive me for being disobedient the times that you told me to witness to others and I did not, out of fear or shame. Lord, I give all of myself to You. I am absolutely nothing without You. I surrender to you my will, my agenda, my thoughts, my desires, my fears, my vulnerabilities, my insecurities, and my way. Lord, empty me so that you can fill me. I love You, thank You, and worship You, for You are everything to me. You are the source of my strength. I know that I can do all things through Christ, who strengthens me, and I praise you, God. In Jesus's name, amen.

Notes